String Ensemble

START POINT

4 TUNES FROM THE SCOTTISH ISLAND OF SANDAY

FOR STRING ENSEMBLE

ED 12975
ISMN M-2201-2692-5
ISBN 978-1-84761-031-7

www.schott-music.com

Mainz · London · Madrid · New York · Paris · Prague · Tokyo · Toronto
© 2007 SCHOTT MUSIC Ltd, London • Printed in Germany

ED 12975
British Library Cataloguing-in-Publication Data.
A catalogue record for this book is available from the British Library

ISMN M-2201-2692-5
ISBN 978-1-84761-031-7

Book design by www.adamhaystudio.com
Music setting by Chris Hinkins
Printed in Germany S&Co.8308

PREFACE

Sir Peter Maxwell Davies has since 1970 made his home in the Orkney Islands. In 1977 he founded the annual St Magnus Festival there, and it has drawn international artists and promoted new music. The emphasis has always been on a strong local participation. Maxwell Davies wrote Start Point for the Sanday Fiddle Club, and it received its first performances at the St Magnus Festival. The four tunes were first performed by the Sanday Fiddle Club, conducted by the composer, at Pickaquoy Centre, Kirkwall, Orkney, as part of the St. Magnus Festival on 21 June 2006. Backaskaill March and Cross Kirk were first performed on the same date of the previous year, conducted by Mike Newman at the Community Hall, Sanday, Orkney, again as part of the St. Magnus Festival. The names of the tunes are names of places on the Orkney Islands.

BIOGRAPHY OF THE COMPOSER

A leading composer on the international arena, Sir Peter Maxwell Davies is also a distinguished conductor and a pioneer in the world of music education. Born in 1934 in Salford, he studied in Manchester and subsequently in Rome and Princeton. From 1959 to 1962, he was Head of Music at Cirencester Grammar School, which launched not only his life-long interest in writing music for non-specialist children to perform, but also initiated the concept of children composing music themselves as part of classroom activities. From 1967 to 1987, Maxwell Davies led his own chamber music ensemble *The Fires of London*, dedicated to performing contemporary music. In 1970 he moved to Orkney (off the north coast of Scotland), and in 1977 founded the annual St Magnus Festival there. Maxwell Davies's compositional output encompasses works for all genres, including eight symphonies, fourteen concertos, and the hugely popular *An Orkney Wedding, with Sunrise*, which was written for the 100th anniversary of the Boston Pops Orchestra, as well as large-scale theatrical works such as the operas *Taverner* and *Resurrection* and the full-length ballets *Salome* and *Caroline Mathilde*.

Start Point
for String Ensemble

Peter Maxwell Davies

1 Start Point

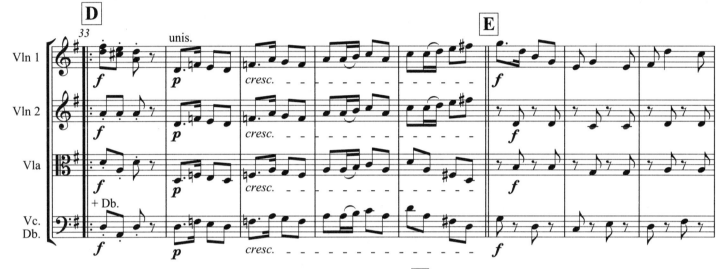

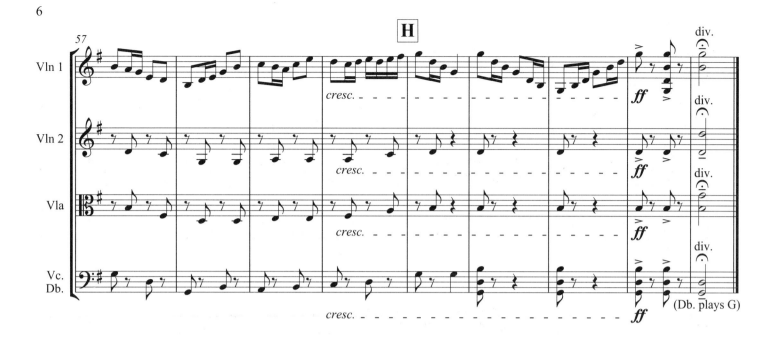

2 Graveshill

Violin 1

Start Point
for String Ensemble

Peter Maxwell Davies

1 Start Point

2 Graveshill

3 Cross Kirk

4 Backaskaill March

9 790220 126932

ISMN M-2201-2693-2 | ED 12975-11

S&Co.8308 Printed in Germany

Start Point
for String Ensemble

Peter Maxwell Davies

1 Start Point

2 Graveshill

3 Cross Kirk

4 Backaskaill March

S&Co.8308 Printed in Germany

9 790220 126949

ISMN M-2201-2694-9 | ED 12975-12

Viola

Start Point
for String Ensemble

Peter Maxwell Davies

1 Start Point

2 Graveshill

3 Cross Kirk

4 Backaskaill March

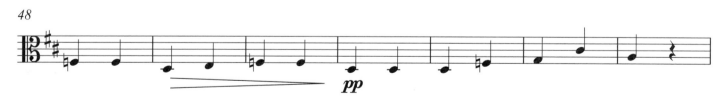

9 790220 126956

ISMN M-2201-2695-6   ED 12975-13

S&Co.8308 Printed in Germany

Violoncello / Double bass (optional)

Start Point
for String Ensemble

Peter Maxwell Davies

1 Start Point

2 Graveshill

3 Cross Kirk

4 Backaskaill March

ISMN M-2201-2696-3 | ED 12975-14

9 790220 126963

S&Co.8308 Printed in Germany

3 Cross Kirk

4 Backaskaill March

12

D.C. alla Coda